Stand Tall!
A book about integrity

Cheri J. Meiners

★

illustrated by Elizabeth Allen

free spirit
PUBLISHING®

Text copyright © 2015 by Cheri J. Meiners, M.Ed.
Illustrations copyright © 2015 by Free Spirit Publishing Inc.

Library of Congress Cataloging-in-Publication Data
Meiners, Cheri J., 1957–
    Stand tall! : a book about integrity / by Cheri J. Meiners ; illustrated by Elizabeth Allen.
        pages cm. — (Being the best me! series)
    ISBN 978-1-57542-484-2 (hard cover) — ISBN 1-57542-484-3 (hard cover) —ISBN 978-1-57542-486-6 (pbk.) — ISBN 1-57542-486-X (pbk.)
1. Integrity—Juvenile literature. 2. Conduct of life—Juvenile literature. I. Allen, Elizabeth (Artist) illustrator. II. Title.
    BJ1533.I58M447 2015
    179'.9—dc23
                                                                                            2014035345

Free Spirit Publishing does not have control over or assume responsibility for author or third-party websites and their content.

Reading Level Grade 1; Interest Level Ages 4–8;
Fountas & Pinnell Guided Reading Level J

Cover and interior design by Tasha Kenyon and Janet LaMere
Edited by Marjorie Lisovskis and Alison Behnke

10 9 8 7 6 5 4 3 2 1
Printed in Hong Kong
P17200215

Free Spirit Publishing Inc.
Minneapolis, MN
(612) 338-2068
help4kids@freespirit.com
www.freespirit.com

To Audrey:
May you always stand tall
and be firmly rooted
in choosing right.

I have a place where I belong.

I'm learning who I am,
and it makes me want to stand tall.

1

Many people care about me
and want to help.

2

I can listen to someone's ideas and then make my own choice.

When I have many choices,
I want to think about each one.

Then I can decide what to do.
Sometimes I can tell by how I feel.

7

I can think about what's important to me,

and then plan what I need to do to make it happen.

I feel peaceful and strong when I make good choices and I don't give up.

11

I show courage
when I make up my own mind

Quick—
grab one!

and do what I think is right.

When someone asks me to help,

Will you help me?

When I do what I say I will,
my words come true.

People can trust me and depend on me.

16

17

I can make good choices even when I'm the only one who knows.

I stand tall when I notice a problem,

20

When I stand up for something important,
I can make the world a little better.

I stand tall when I
encourage someone
and let that person shine.

I show respect when I let people know that they are important.

What I do matters.
I feel needed
when I'm part of things
that are bigger than I am.

Being kind is always
the right thing to do.

I try to act the way I want people
to act with me.

I am the only one like me.

I plan to stand tall
and be my very best.

Ways to Reinforce the Ideas in *Stand Tall!*

Stand Tall! teaches integrity—a quality of dependability, moral courage, and resoluteness. At its core, integrity is a person's strong sense of self and values, and the fortitude to act in accordance with those values—even when it's difficult or unpopular to do so. From this book, children learn the importance of being committed to their ideas and beliefs, and following through on their intentions. A life of integrity can influence others in many positive ways. Being dependable and standing up for beliefs can influence others to make wise choices. A desire to help others can have a wide impact.

Without integrity, other qualities—such as intelligence, creativity, or having lots of energy—can be misdirected. Though it's sometimes challenging, being true to yourself and your sense of right is the basis for strong character. It can lead to improved mental health, greater feelings of fulfillment, improved relationships, and a greater sense of purpose in a person's life—all of which can lead to greater happiness. Children can learn integrity by becoming more familiar with their own patterns of thinking, and by adopting some of the principles discussed in this book and supported by the activities on pages 33–35.

Words to know:

Here are terms you may want to discuss.

choice: a decision; a chance to choose from different possibilities

courage: bravery; when you show courage you do something you believe is right, even if it is hard

decide: to make up your mind

depend: to count on someone to do something, and believe that the person will do it

encourage: to support and reassure someone; to help someone feel confident

integrity: being true to yourself and other people by knowing and doing what you think is right

peaceful: calm; not worried

promise: to say that you will do something and really mean it; when you keep a promise, you do what you say you will do

respect: to treat others kindly and politely; to know and show that a person is important

shine: to stand out; when you let other people shine, you let them have attention and a chance to show what they can do well

stand tall: to be brave and proud and strong in doing what you think is right

trust: to believe that someone is telling the truth and will do what he or she says

As you read each spread, ask children:

- What is happening in this picture?
- What is the main idea?
- How would you feel if you were this person?

Here are additional questions you might discuss:

> **Note:** *Before this discussion, you may want to start by introducing and explaining the word* integrity. *For example, you could say,* "When you have integrity, you do what you know is right. When we talk about 'standing tall,' we mean integrity."

Pages 1–9

- What does it mean to belong? Where is a place where you belong?
- What are some ways you are learning who you are?
- What does it mean to stand tall? What are some ways you stand tall?
- Who are some of the people who care about you? How do they help you or show you that they care?
- When you have choices, why does it help to think and learn about those choices? How do you decide what to do?

- What is something important that you want to do? What can you do now to plan and get ready to do it?

Pages 10–19

- Tell about a time when you wanted to give up on something hard, but you kept going.

- Think of a time you made good choices and stood tall. What did you do? Was it easy or hard? How did you feel afterward?

- What is a time when you made up your own mind about what was the right thing to do? How did you decide what to do?

- When someone asks you for help, what do you say? What do you do? How do you feel when you help someone?

- Tell about a time when you said you would do something for another person, and then you did it. How does doing what you say you will do help people trust you?

- Think of a time you tried to fix a problem by yourself, without being asked. What did you do? *(Examples: helped a sibling, did a household chore.)* How did you feel when you took care of a situation by yourself?

Pages 20–31

- What are important things that you want to stand up for? When you stand tall, how do you think people around you feel?

- When did you encourage someone else in something they were doing? How did the person feel? How did you feel? What are ways that you can encourage other people?

- What does it mean to be part of something that is bigger than you? *(Examples: To do something that helps others; to be part of a group, such as a family, a class, or a sport; to do things that are with, and for, other people.)* What are some good things you do that are bigger than you? *(Examples: Be a class helper; draw a picture for a friend; set the table for dinner.)* How does it feel when you do these things?

- Do you agree that being kind is always the right thing to do? Why?

- Why do you think it's a good idea to act the way you like people to act with you?

- What is something that you do that helps you stand tall? *(Examples: I don't take things that aren't mine; I try to help when someone asks me; I do things I'm assigned to do, such as make my bed.)*

Integrity Activities and Games

Read this book often with your child or group of children. Once children are familiar with the book, refer to it when teachable moments arise involving both positive behavior and problems relating to dependability, perseverance, commitment, and trustworthiness. In addition, use the following activities to reinforce children's understanding of integrity and standing tall.

Heroes Who Stand Tall

Directions: Read about people who have shown integrity throughout history. Talk with children about what these people did and how they stood tall. Ask and discuss questions like "What did the person do to stand tall?" and "After learning and thinking about this person, what new ideas do you have for how you can stand tall?"

Extension: Have children draw a picture of something a person from history has done to show integrity. Have children talk about their picture and explain why this is an example of standing tall. They might also talk about something that they could do to show integrity.

Variation: Invite children to choose heroes from their own families. Ask children to talk to their parents and other family members regarding their family history and heritage. Children may learn how family members have stood tall in the past, while also talking about the family's hopes for the future. Knowing about family history can help children build self-esteem, make wise choices, and develop integrity.

Stand Tall and Follow the Leader

Directions: Have children stand up. Direct children to follow what you say—which may be different from what you do. Call out various actions such as "Jump up and down" or "Clap your hands." Start out by doing the same action that you call out. Then start interspersing different actions than the directions you call out. (For instance, you might say, "Touch your shoulders" while touching your elbows instead.) Children sit down if they don't follow your verbal directions.

Discussion: Talk about how it was easier for children to follow your actions when you were saying the same thing that you were doing. If a leader says one thing and does something else, it is hard to trust him or her. People who stand tall and have integrity are true to their words. Other people trust those who do the things they say they will do.

Flags Waving Tall

Materials: White paper and markers or white handkerchiefs and fabric paint; wooden dowels, skewers, or craft sticks (optional)

Directions: Ask children to imagine having their own country. Have them think about how they would want people to act in their country. What is the one, most important rule they would make to remind everyone to stand tall and be their best? *(Examples: Treat everyone fairly. Respect yourself and other people. Know what's right, and do it.)*

After talking about these rules, have children make flags that represent their rules. They may choose to use pictures, words, or both. Hang the flags on the wall, or mount them to dowels and "fly" them as a reminder to children to stand tall and stay true to their own most important rules and beliefs.

Exercises in Standing Tall

Directions: Stand with children in a gym or other indoor space with room to move. Have children imagine that they are the things that you describe. As they move and imagine (or afterward), talk about how each of these things can remind us to stand tall and be firm in our choices and actions. Here are some examples:

- **Tree:** Have children do the "tree" yoga pose, balancing by resting one foot just above or below the knee of the opposite leg. Have children imagine themselves planting their feet firmly as if they are growing roots below the floor that are keeping them firm. Later, talk about how this pose represents the idea of standing tall and strong—doing what's right and not letting yourself be swayed by outside pressures. Have children share what their "roots" are—the people or things in their lives that help them make good decisions.

- **Mountain:** Have children find and hold their own poses representing a strong, unmoving mountain.

Stand Tall Scenarios

Preparation: On individual 3" x 5" index cards, write the following sample scenarios, writing one scenario on each card. You can also add your own. Stack the cards face down, or put them in a bag or other container for children to draw from.

Sample Stand Tall Scenarios

- Marcus is playing at his friend's house, and they have spread toys all over the floor. Marcus finds out that he is leaving in just a few minutes.

- Grace forgot to do her homework.

- While Hector was bringing his grandmother's dishes to the sink, he dropped a bowl and it broke.

- Isabella is playing outside and sees a neighbor carrying two bags of groceries as she walks to her apartment.

- Rosa borrowed her friend's crayons, and she lost one.

- Asad noticed that his little brother was sad when his block tower fell down.

- Mikaela bought something at the store and the person accidentally gave her too much money back as change.

- Hiro's mom asks him to clean his room, but he wants to play with his friend.
- On the playground at school, Sam sees some classmates being mean to another child.
- At lunchtime, Saafi is about to sit with her friends when she notices that a new student is sitting alone.

Directions

Level 1

Have children stand while you read a scenario from a card. Then provide a short ending—positive or negative—to the scenario. (Example: For the scenario "Rosa borrowed her friend's crayons, and she lost one," possible endings might be: *Rosa decided not to tell her friend; Rosa offered to give her friend one of her crayons;* or *Rosa apologized.*) If children feel that the child in the scenario acted with integrity in the situation you've described, they will stand tall with their shoulders back and heads up. If they think the scenario depicts a poor choice, they might put their heads down, slump shoulders, and lower their eyes.

Level 2

After reading a scenario, ask, "What might this child do to stand tall?" Call on a child to give a standing tall response. Other children may clap if they agree. Prompt children as needed to give appropriate responses.

Level 3

Place children in pairs or small groups. Read a scenario to each group. Ask them to talk together about what they would do in the situation, and to role-play their responses. Allow time for each small group to come up with a standing tall response, and then have groups perform their scenarios for the larger group. Discuss how the situation was handled, and whether the children showed integrity in responding to the problem.

Stand Tall: Superheroes to the Rescue

Materials: 3" x 5" index cards, pen; superhero costume pieces (optional) such as a towel or blanket for a cape and an eye mask made from black construction paper and string; camera or phone with video capability (optional)

Preparation: Make Superhero cards by writing scenarios on index cards in response to the discussion question, "How can *you* be a hero to someone?" Possible scenarios include: Get a glass of water for someone who is thirsty; help set or clear the table at dinner; open the door for a person at a store; show an adult how to use features on a phone or other device; feed a pet; help a parent look for a misplaced item like keys or glasses.

Discuss: Using optional pictures or toy figures, talk about children's favorite superheroes and how these heroes stand tall. Possible prompts for discussion include: "Why do you think this person is a hero?" "What does the superhero do to stand tall?" "How can *you* be a hero to someone?" Explain that even through small, everyday actions, you can be a hero if you are doing something that helps someone, and makes things better for others.

Level 1

A child draws a Superhero scenario card. Role-play a scenario with that child as the superhero. If desired, the child can wear a costume for the part. The child can choose another child to help with the skit. Give each child an opportunity to be the hero.

Level 2

Ask the child who is dressed as the superhero, "How can *you* be a hero to someone?" Invite another child to do a skit with the child. Have them come up with an idea for their skit, possibly drawing from the examples that were used in Level 1.

Level 3

Using the Stand Tall cards from the preceding activity, let the child choose a scenario and tell or act out how a superhero would respond to the challenge.

Extension: You may wish to practice and videotape each skit. Have a movie day or evening with optional snacks and invite an audience to see the newest superhero movies.